Mother Tapley's Recipe Book:
Vintage Cooking

Katherine E. Tapley-Milton

Published by

4 Paws Games and Publishing

Bruno, Saskatchewan, Canada

Mother Tapley's Recipe Book: Vintage Cooking

Book # 2 in the series

Written and Created by Katherine E. Tapley-Milton
Photos by Katherine E. Tapley-Milton

Cover Art by 4 Paws Games and Publishing

Edited by Katherine E. Tapley-Milton and 4 Paws Games and Publishing

Formatted and Published by 4 Paws Games and Publishing
Published 2017 First Edition
ISBN 13: 978-1-988345-84-0

Attention: Permission C/O
Katherine E. Tapley-Milton
18 Squire Street
Sackville, New Brunswick E4L 4K9

DEPARTMENT OF JUSTICE
FBI ANTI-PIRACY WARNING
FIDELITY BRAVERY INTEGRITY AUTHORITY
FEDERAL BUREAU OF INVESTIGATION

Other Books by Katherine E. Tapley-Milton
Big Stuff in the Maritimes Series
1-3

Other Books
Kathy's Down East Christmas Cookbook
Mother Tapley's Recipe Book: Vintage Cooking
The Disappearing Mailboxes of New Brunswick and Nova
Scotia: A Touring of Mailboxes
Old Boats and Old Quotes
The Adventures of the Three Mouse-Breath-Kateers
The Adventures of Sir Lancelot the Cat
Scintillating Scarecrows
And more.

Find Katherine Online
Website
http://authorkatherinetapleymilton.weebly.com

Facebook
https://www.facebook.com/KatherineETapleyMilton

Amazon Authors Central Page
https://www.amazon.com/Katherine-Tapley-
Milton/e/B00CP8EBR8

Like the book? Please post a review online where you bought
it!

TABLE OF CONTENTS

FOREWORD

My mother lived to be over 101 years old and she gave me all
her cookbooks. These are stick-to-your-ribs recipes that we
grew up with. I think that some of these old recipes are brilliant
in their simplicity.

APPETIZERS

Cheese Log

Ingredients:

1/2 lbs of cream cheese

3 tbsp mayonnaise

2 tbsp minced onion

2 tbsp minced green pepper

3 stuffed olives, chopped

1/3 cup crushed soda crackers

Instructions:

Cream together 1/2 lbs of cream cheese and 3 tbsp of mayonnaise. Mix ingredients completely and shape into a long log. Wrap it in wax paper, chilling until stiff (which is about 3 hours).

Serve with fresh, crisp crackers.

Chicken-Almond Tempters

Ingredients:

3/4 cup finely chopped chicken

1/4 chopped almonds

1-1/2 tbsp mayonnaise

pinch of pepper and salt

Instructions:

Mix completely. Spread crackers or bread with mayonnaise and top with chicken mixture. Garnish with parsley.

This recipe should make 24 appetizers.

Green Onion Appetizer

Ingredients:

1 cup of sour cream

3 tbsp minced green onion

1/4 salt

1 tbsp pimentos finely chopped

Instructions:

Cover the bowl and chill, so that the flavor will blend. Spread on crackers, or chips.

Shrimp Tempters

Ingredients:

4-1/2 oz of shrimp, finely cut up

3 tbsp mayonnaise

1 tbsp finely cut up green pepper

1 tsp lemon juice

some drops of tabasco sauce to taste

Instructions:

Put the shrimp mixture on chips, crackers, or toast. A pickle can be put on top.

This recipe makes 24 appetizers.

Maraschino Cheese Ball

Ingredients:

1 brick of cream cheese

20 maraschino cherries, finely chopped

1 finely chopped pecan

Instructions:

Take cream cheese and soften it by mixing. Put cherries in and mix again. Form in little balls and dip into the nuts. Place in the fridge until firm.

Addictive Nibblers

Ingredients:

potato chips

different kinds of small crackers

parmesan cheese

Instructions:

Spread chips and crackers on a cookie sheet with parchment paper underneath. Put a generous amount of Parmesan cheese on top. Bake in preheated 400°F oven for 2-3 minutes or until golden brown.

Fruit Cocktail Supreme

Ingredients:

2 cups of pineapple chunks

mint, minced and put in the fruit

1-1/2 cups of peaches, cut coarsely

1 cup halved red seedless grapes

1 large, red apple

Instructions:

Chop the apple up and combine it with the other fruit.

Cover and chill in the refrigerator to let the flavours blend.

When serving, pour orange juice over the fruit.

Serves 6-8 people.

Paradise Cocktail

Ingredients:

mandarin oranges

pineapple chunks

pineapple juice

Instructions:

Take an equal part of Mandarin and pineapple chunks and pour pineapple juice over them. Sprinkle with sugar or Stevia®. This mixture would be nice over sherbet or sorbet.

Melon Ball Delight

Ingredients:

cantaloupe

honeydew melon

watermelon

ginger ale

Instructions:

Take all the fruit and make balls out of them with a melon baller. Pour ginger ale over the melons.

Chill completely and garnish with a Maraschino cherry, a sprig of mint, or a fresh strawberry when served in individual dishes.

Skyscraper Canape

Ingredients:

6 rounds of bread

1/2 cup of devilled ham

3/4 cup of mayonnaise

lettuce leaves, fresh

3 tomatoes, sliced

1 green pepper

6 slices of cucumber

6 stuffed olives

1 tsp capers

1 tbsp horseradish

Instructions:

Toast bread and make rounds of it by cutting off the crust.
How many rounds you make depends on how many guests
that you expect. On the unbuttered side put devilled ham
mixed with 1/4 cup of mayonnaise. Arrange on lettuce
leaves.

Peel tomatoes and put a thick slice on each round. Put green
pepper rings on top of the tomato. Next a slice of cucumber
goes over the pepper.

Finally, top with stuffed olives and some capers. Garnish
with the remains of the mayonnaise and horseradish.

Apple and Salami Porcupine

Ingredients:

1 large red apple

1/4 lbs of unsliced salami

3 dozen pickled onions

Instructions:

Wash and dry the apple. Cut the salami into 1/2" cubes. Alternate onion and salami on the toothpick and stick into apple. Keep doing this until the apple looks like a porcupine.

Put on a plate and the guests can help themselves.

Potato Chip Snappers

Ingredients:

1/2 cup of spreading blue cheese

1 tsp minced onion

Instructions:

Mix together cheese and onion and put in a bowl. Provide a larger bowl with potato chips, so guests can dip in the spread.

Stuffed Celery Stalks

Ingredients:

crisp celery stalks 2-1/2" to 3" long

1 pkg cream cheese

1/4 cup of canned, crushed pineapple

1 tbsp pimento

Instructions:

Blend ingredients and stuff the celery stalks.

Alternatively, for a different taste you can mix cream cheese with 1 tsp each of horseradish, minced chives, 1/4 tsp of lemon juice. This can be used to stuff celery stalks.

BEVERAGES

Cranberry Lemonade Refresher

Ingredients:

2 bottles cranberry juice

1 bottle lemonade

Instructions:

Mix ingredients together. Chill for at least an hour before serving.

Tangerine Bubbly

Ingredients:

tangerine juice

ginger ale

Instructions:

Mix equal parts of tangerine juice with ginger ale. Chill well before serving.

Fruit Refresher

Ingredients:

grape juice

lime pop

Instructions:

Mix 1-part grape juice and 3 parts lime pop. Chill well, then serve.

Banana Crush

Ingredients:

2 bananas

1 small can of lemonade

1 small can of frozen orange juice

1 small can of pineapple juice

1/2 small can of apricot nectar

1-1/4 cups of sugar

3 cups of water

7-Up®

Instructions:

Mash bananas in a pan and add the juices. Boil the sugar and water together until dissolved. Add this to the juice mixture, stirring well.

Freeze, stirring from time to time while freezing to a slush consistency. Fill glasses half with slush and half with 7-Up®.

SOUPS AND CHOWDERS

St. Germain Soup

Ingredients:

1 can of peas

1/2 onion

1 bay leaf

sprig of parsley

pinch of nutmeg

1 cup of milk

1/2 tsp sugar

1 tsp salt

3 cups of chicken broth

1 tbsp butter

1 tbsp cornstarch

whipped cream

Instructions:

Mix seasonings with peas and simmer for half an hour. Mash and add chicken stock. Boil. Strain and thicken with butter and cornstarch while boiling. Add the milk, seasonings, and top with cream.

Pioneer Soup

Ingredients:

1-1/2 lbs of spare ribs

6 medium potatoes

1/2 cup of tomatoes

3 onions, sliced thin

salt and pepper to taste

Instructions:

Put the ribs on the stove in a pot of cold water. When they come to a boil, skim.

Boil for half an hour, then add onions, and tomatoes.

After another half hour add salt and pepper and potatoes and simmer.

When everything is cooked, serve hot.

Lobster Chowder

Ingredients:

2 cups of lobster meat, chopped

1 medium onion, chopped

2 medium potatoes, chopped

2 cups of milk

1 cup of light cream

butter the size of an egg

1 tsp salt (maybe less if the lobster is salty)

1/4 tsp pepper

1 cup of boiling water

Instructions:

In water cook onion and potatoes until soft. Put in lobster meat and season with salt and pepper. Heat to boiling and then boil for 5 minutes.

Next add milk, cream, and butter, heating to the point of boiling.

Serve hot with home made rolls or biscuits.

Duchess Soup

Ingredients:

2 tbsp Minute® tapioca

1 tsp salt

1 tbsp shredded onion

1 litre of milk

1 beaten egg yolk

2 tbsp butter

1/4 cup of grated cheese

1/2 tsp Worcestershire sauce

2 tbsp chopped parsley

whipped cream

Instructions:

Put milk, tapioca, salt, and onion in the top of double boiler. Cook until it is clear. Add butter, cheese, seasoning, and egg yolk. Remove from stove. Add parsley and serve. Top with some whipped cream.

Cream of Cauliflower Soup

Ingredients:

2 cups cauliflower, finely chopped

4 cups of milk

1 tbsp butter

1-1/2 tbsp cornstarch

Instructions:

Cook cauliflower and milk until cauliflower is soft. Strain it through a coarse sieve. Return to the stove and add seasonings, butter, and cornstarch. Put a little cold milk in and stir until smooth in texture. Cook until thickened and serve hot. Make sure not to burn the milk on the bottom.

Brown Cabbage Soup

Ingredients:

Soup bone (3-4 lbs)

2 Quarts of cold water

2 tsp salt

1/4 tsp pepper

1 bay leaf

1/2 medium cabbage head

2 medium onions

1 cup of chopped celery

1 cup of chopped beet tops

1 tbsp fat or oil

Instructions:

Cover bone with water and add salt, pepper, and bay leaf. Boil for 1 and a half hours. Cut cabbage into eights and cook with remaining vegetables in fat or oil. Brown well. Add to stock and bone and cook for 3/4 hour. Take meat from bone and add to soup.

Serves 8. May be served with clotted cream or whipped cream.

Henny Penny Soup

Ingredients:

1 stewing hen

3 liters of water

2 tsp salt

white pepper

1 bay leaf

1 sprig of parsley

12 leeks, white part only

2 tbsp uncooked rice

Instructions:

Cover hen and spices in the water. Put in the sliced leeks. Boil, then simmer for 3 hours.

Take the chicken out of the pot and skim off the fat. This can be done easily, if you put it in a freezer and wait until the fat gets hard. Just lift the fat off. Put back in the pot and add the remaining leeks and rice. Simmer for half an hour.

Remove everything off the chicken but keep the light and dark meat. Cut fine and add to soup.

Serves 6.

Polish Barley Soup

Ingredients:

3/4 cup of pearl barley

8 cups of bouillon

1/2 cup of butter or other fat

2 onions, chopped

2 carrots, chopped

1 turnip, chopped

1 leek, chopped

1/2 cup of chopped celery

2/3 cup of canned mushrooms, chopped

1 tsp salt

1/8 tsp pepper

4 tbsp sour cream

Instructions:

In 1-1/2 cup of bouillon simmer barley until soft. Boil vegetables until tender in the remaining bouillon, then add barley and seasonings.

Serve hot with a dollop of sour cream.

Serves 6.

Shrimp Bisque

Ingredients:

2 cups of cooked shrimp

2 tbsp butter

1 tbsp diced carrot

2 tbsp diced celery

2 tbsp chopped mushrooms

1 tbsp of minced onion

3/4 tsp salt

pinch of cayenne pepper

1 cup of chicken bouillon

1/2 cup of cream

1/2 cup of sauterne (French sweet wine)

Instructions:

Take shrimp and shell them, cutting them in pieces. Melt butter and put shrimp, and vegetables in, cooking slowly for 3 minutes.

Add seasonings and bouillon and cook for 20 minutes. Rub through a coarse sieve; add cream and sauterne and heat to boiling. Garnish with a dollop of whipped cream.

Cream of Chicken Soup

Ingredients:

3 tbsp rice

1/2 cup diced celery

3 cups of chicken bouillon

2 cups of hot milk

salt and pepper

chopped parsley

Ingredients:

In stock, cook rice and celery until soft. Drain and rub though a sieve.

Incorporate with milk and season to taste. Garnish with parsley and serve hot.

Serves 4-6.

Baked Bean Soup

Ingredients:

3 slices of bacon, diced

2 cups of baked or boiled beans

4 cups of cold water

1 tbsp flour

1 tbsp fat

1 tbsp salt

dash of pepper

pinch of paprika

Instructions:

Cook bacon thoroughly, then add beans and cold water.
Cook until the beans are soft, then rub through a coarse sieve.
Return to heat and add a bit more water, if needed. Blend in
flour, fat, salt, pepper, and paprika. Cook 2-3 more minutes,
stirring constantly.

Wine Soup

Ingredients:

7/8 cup of barley

3 liters of water

1 cup of seedless raisins

1 cup of sugar

1 stick of cinnamon

1/4 cup of citron, minced

1 pint of grape wine or sherry

Instructions:

Put barley in water overnight to soften it. Make sure that the water covers it. Boil until tender, which could take an hour. Incorporate raisins, sugar, citron, and cinnamon. Cook for half an hour more.

Add grape wine or sherry and cook 5 more minutes. Serve chilled.

Serves 8-10.

MAIN COURSES

Sailor's Pie

Ingredients:

1 large onion

2 cups of streamed or canned clams, minced

1/2 tsp salt

2 tbsp fat

2 cups of cubed, cooked potatoes

pinch of pepper

pastry

Instructions:

Chop onion and cook in fat until brown and tender. Add clams, potatoes, and seasonings to taste. Heat and put into a baking dish. Put pastry over the ingredients 1/8" thick. Prick holes with a fork so that steam can escape. Bake at 400°F for 20 minutes or until golden brown.

Scotch Mince

Ingredients:

1-1/2 lbs of round, ground steak

2 medium sized onions

2 tbsp butter

flour

pepper

2 cups of hot water

Instructions:

Cover the meat with flour. Sprinkle seasonings on it. Melt butter in a hot fry pan and then put the meat in. Keep turning meat over until golden brown. Add hot water, onions, and simmer 1/2 to 3/4 hours. When done, serve with mashed potatoes and a green vegetable such as peas or beans.

Serves 6.

Potato Croquettes

Ingredients:

2 cups of hot mashed potatoes

2 tbsp of butter

1/2 tsp salt

pinch of cayenne pepper

few drops of onion juice

1 tsp finely chopped parsley

bread crumbs

Instructions:

Mix ingredients in the order given and beat thoroughly.

Shape, then roll in crumbs.

Fry until lightly browned in deep fat and drain on brown paper.

Shrimp or Lobster Salad

Ingredients:

1 head of lettuce

green peas

boiled potatoes, diced

mayonnaise

2 cans of shrimp

Instructions:

Put lettuce leaves in a bowl and put a modest amount of mayonnaise on the leaves. Make a layer of diced potatoes, peas, shrimp. Repeat the layers. On top put a small amount of mayonnaise and chopped lettuce.

Russian Meatloaf

Ingredients:

1 lbs of hamburger

3 medium onions

1 cup of rice

1 can of peas

1 can of tomato soup

Instructions:

Fry onions until golden brown and soft. Remove from heat. Brown the hamburger. Cook the rice until it is soft.

In a casserole dish put a layer of meat, a layer of rice, a layer of peas, a layer of onions until the ingredients are used up.

Pour tomato soup over the top and cook at 350°F for an hour.

Corn Souffle

Ingredients:

1 can of corn

1 tbsp of butter

1 cup of milk

1 tsp salt

2 tbsp flour

2 eggs

pepper to taste

Instructions:

Melt butter and add flour and pour milk on gradually. Bring to a boiling point. Next, add corn, seasonings, egg yolks and stiffly beaten egg whites. Bake for half an hour in a moderate oven.

Baked Mac and Cheese

Ingredients:

1 pkg of macaroni

1/2 lbs of cheese

1 green pepper, minced

1 can of tomatoes

1 onion, minced

1 well-beaten egg

salt and pepper to taste

Instructions:

Cook macaroni in boiling, salted water until tender, then drain. Grate the cheese, mince the green pepper, and mix with macaroni, tomatoes, onion, egg, and seasonings.

Leave some cheese for the top.

Place in casserole dish and cover with cheese. Bake at 350°F until golden brown.

Boston Baked Beans

Ingredients:

4 cups of white beans

1/2 tsp soda

1 tbsp mustard

1/4 cup of molasses

1 tbsp salt

1/3 tsp pepper

1 cup of water

1 onion

1 apple cored

1/2 lbs of bacon

Instructions:

Wash beans and soak overnight.

Parboil with soda and wash again.

Place beans in covered bean pot or roaster pan with mustard, molasses, salt, pepper, and water, making a well in centre for onion and apple.

Lay strips of bacon on top on top and bake in a slow oven of 225°F for 6-8 hours.

Scalloped Ham and Potatoes

Ingredients:

1 thick slice of ham

4 cups of potatoes

2 small onions

2 tbsp all-purpose flour

salt and pepper to taste

2 cups of milk

Instructions:

Cut ham in 6 pieces. Place 1/3 of potatoes in greased casserole over the ham. Put sliced onion, sprinkled flour, seasonings and layer all ingredients. Top with potatoes and pour milk over everything.

Bake for one hour in 350°F oven for 30 minutes or until potato is soft. If salty ham is used, omit the salt from the recipe.

Beef Upside-Down Pie

Ingredients:

1-1/2 cups of flour

3 tsp baking powder

1/2 tsp salt

1 tsp paprika

1/4 tsp pepper

2 tbsp shortening

1/4 cup of milk

1 sliced onion

1 can of tomato soup

1 lbs of Hamburger

Instructions:

Cut the shortening into the flour and add milk. Set this aside. Cook the onion in the shortening.

Add the can of tomato soup, add salt, and hamburger together. Bring to a boil and spread the first mixture on top.

Bake in a hot oven at 425°F for 20 minutes. Remove from oven and put upside down on a warmed plate.

Chicken Puff

Ingredients:

1-1/2 cups of flour

2 tsp baking powder

2 egg whites, beaten

1 cup of milk

1 cup of chicken, minced

2 tsp onion, minced

1/4 cup of grated carrot

2 tbsp melted butter

1-1/2 cups of chicken gravy

salt to taste

Instructions:

In a bowl, sift together flour, baking powder, and salt. Add egg yolks and milk into the mixture. Add chicken, onion, carrot, and butter. Mix well. Fold in beaten egg whites (beaten stiff). Bake in a hot oven at 400°F until vegetables are soft and the crust is brown.

Serve with chicken gravy.

Spanish Rice

Ingredients:

1/2 cup of rice

1-1/2 lbs of hamburger, steak, or leftover meat

1/2 cup of grated cheese

1 can of tomato soup or canned tomatoes

1 small onion

salt and pepper to taste

Instructions:

First cook rice in boiling water with a little salt in it. This should take 10 minutes. Drain the rice with a strainer and run cold water through it.

Add meat, cheese, tomatoes or soup, onion, and seasonings. Bake at 375°F until golden brown.

Almond Chicken Casserole

Ingredients:

1/2 large, white onion

butter or margarine

1/2 cup fresh mushrooms

2 tbsp flour

2 cups of milk

2 tbsp butter

1 tsp summer savoury

3-4 cups of diced cooked chicken

bread crumbs

Instructions:

Cook onion in butter leaving half cooked. Add mushrooms and cook until slightly undercooked. In a separate pot mix flour and milk, add butter, and cook over low heat. Add summer savoury, and salt and pepper to taste. If the mixture is too thick add more milk. Put chicken pieces in and heat until warm.

Pour into a casserole dish and distribute almonds and bread crumbs and a dash of summer savoury on top. Bake in a 275°F oven for 25 minutes.

Chinese Casserole

Ingredients:

1-1/2 cups of cooked rice

1 lbs hamburger

2 medium onions, chopped

1 lbs can of bean sprouts or equivalent fresh ones

1/4 green pepper, chopped

1 cup of fresh mushrooms

1 cup of beef bouillon

1/3 cup of soya sauce

1/2 cup of water

1/2 tsp ginger

Instructions:

Cook the hamburger and when it is done add the bean sprouts and mushrooms and cook slightly. Mix all the ingredients together and put in greased casserole dish. Bake at 425°F for 40 minutes.

Chinese Laundry

Ingredients:

2 lbs of hamburger, lightly browned

1 layer of onions, sliced and lightly fried

2 cups of pre-cooked rice

1 can of chicken soup

1 cup of mushrooms

bean sprouts

water chestnuts

1 can of cream of mushroom soup

Instructions:

Layer the ingredients in a buttered casserole dish. Over the top put 1/4 cup of soya sauce and 1/4 cup of water. Bake at 375°F for half an hour.

Crustless Quiche

Ingredients:

1 pkg of chopped broccoli thawed and rinsed

3 cups of grated Cheddar cheese

1-1/2 cups of chopped ham

2/3 cup chopped onion

1-1/3 cups of milk

3 eggs

3/4 cup of Bisquick®, sifted

3/4 tsp salt

1/2 tsp pepper

Instructions:

Mix together milk, eggs, and Bisquick®. Pour over meat, onion, broccoli, and cheese. Pour ingredients into a pie plate. Bake at 400°F for 30-40 minutes. Put in oven again to melt the cheese for 2-3 minutes. The crust is formed by the Bisquick®.

Delmonico Potatoes

Ingredients:

4 tbsp butter

4 tbsp flour

1/2 cup grated cheese

2 cups of milk

cold, boiled potatoes cut in cubes

Instructions:

Melt butter and add flour and cheese. Add milk gradually and bring to a boil. Fill greased baking dish with alternating layers of potatoes and sauce and bake in 350°F oven for 30 minutes. Top with buttered crumbs and reheat in the oven.

Witches Brew

Ingredients:

1-1/2 hamburger steak

1/4 lbs of bacon, cut up

2 large Spanish onions

2 large sweet peppers

1 pkg of sautéed mushrooms

1 can of kidney beans

2 cups egg noodles, rice, or spaghetti

3 large ripe tomatoes

salt and pepper to taste

Instructions:

Fry steak until nicely brown, then fry the bacon and add to steak.

Add onions and peppers which are minced. Cook for 10 minutes.

Add mushrooms, beans, noodles, or rice, or spaghetti. Thinly slice tomatoes. Mix well and simmer for 20 minutes. If desired, ingredients can be placed in greased casserole dish and grated cheese, bread crumbs, and bacon can be placed on top and browned in the oven. The bacon is not added to the steak in this case.

Goulash

Ingredients:

1 lbs of spaghetti, cooked

2 lbs of hamburger

1/2 lbs of cheese

4 cups of tomatoes

1 can of pimentos

3 medium-sized onions

1/2 lbs butter

Salt

Instructions:

Combine all ingredients and heat very slowly on the top of the stove.

Chicken Loaf

Ingredients:

2 cups of cooked chicken

1 cup of soft bread crumbs

2 tbsp chopped parsley

2 tbsp chopped celery

2/3 tsp salt

2 eggs

1 cup of milk

3 tbsp melted butter

Instructions:

Combine all ingredients and pour into a greased loaf pan.

Bake for 30 minutes in 375°F oven.

Take out of the mold and serve in slices.

Family Meatloaf

Ingredients:

1-1/2 lbs of hamburger

1 beaten egg

1 cup of rolled oats

1 cup of milk

1-1/2 tsp minced onion

1/2 tsp dried parsley flakes

1-1/2 tsp salt

1/8 tsp pepper

1 tsp Worcestershire sauce

Instructions:

Combine all ingredients thoroughly and pack lightly into a 9" x 5" loaf pan. Put three diagonal slashes across the top and fill with 3 tbsp ketchup. Bake in 350°F oven for 1-1/4 to 1-1/2 hours.

Serves 6-8.

SAUCES, SPREADS, AND DRESSINGS

Cream Cheese and Egg Spread

Ingredients:

1 3 oz pkg of cream cheese

4 hard, cooked eggs yolks

1 tsp vinegar

2 tsp prepared mustard

1/8 tsp salt

1/8 tsp paprika

1 tbsp minced green pepper

Instructions:

Combine all ingredients. This is a good use for leftover eggs yolks.

Cocktail Sauce

Ingredients:

1 tbsp ketchup

1/2 tsp lemon juice

1/4 tsp Worcestershire sauce

1 tsp prepared horseradish

1/2 tsp olive oil

1/2 tsp finely chopped onion

1/2 tsp celery salt

1/2 tsp minced green pepper

Instructions:

Combine ingredients in the order they are written and chill completely. This sauce may be used for lobster, crabmeat, scallops, and shrimps. The amount is only for one serving.

SALADS

What is a honeymoon salad?

Lettuce alone.

Orange Jell-O Salad

Ingredients:

3 oz orange Jell-O®

1 cup of boiling water

1 can of mandarin oranges, drained

1/4 cup of evaporated milk

1/2 cup of mayonnaise

1/2 cup of cottage cheese

Instructions:

Pour water over Jell-O® and when thickened slightly add oranges, milk, and mayonnaise. Cool, but don't let it get too thick. Stir in cottage cheese. Put in jelly mould and let set.

Serves 5-6.

Banana and Celery Salad

Ingredients:

6 pieces of celery

6 tbsp peanut butter

lettuce

6 small bananas

3/4 cup of mayonnaise

Small amount of whipped cream

Instructions:

Stuff celery with peanut butter and cut into small pieces.
Arrange on beds of lettuce with bananas sliced or diced. Serve
with mayonnaise to which whip cream may be added.

Mom's Frozen Salad

Ingredients:

2 tbsp Sugar

2 tbsp Miracle Whip®

8 oz can of whole cranberries

10 oz pineapple chunks

1/2 cup chopped walnut

6 oz cream, whipped

Instructions:

Cream sugar, Miracle Whip, and cheese. Add cranberries, pineapple, and walnuts. Fold in cream. Put in mould and freeze.

Black Eyed Susan Salad

Ingredients:

large oranges

figs, diced

chopped celery

fruit salad dressing (homemade or store bought)

Instructions:

Separate the oranges into sections, allowing half of one for each person.

Mix figs with celery and moisten slightly with fruit salad dressing.

Season orange sections with salad dressing and arrange like Black-eyed Susan petals on individual plates. Form centres with fig mixture and garnish salad with tips of celery.

Sunshine Salad

Ingredients:

2 envelopes of gelatin

1/4 cup of water

1 cup of cold orange juice

1/4 sugar

1/2 tsp salt

juice of lemons

14 oz tin of pineapple

10 oz tin of mandarin oranges

1/2 cup of celery cut diagonally

Instructions:

Dissolve gelatin in water. Heat orange juice to boiling point, adding gelatin slowly. Next add salt and lemon juice. Cool. Add fruit and carrots and celery. Pour all the mixture and put into gelatin mould. Place in fridge. When set, turn out on a plate. Decorate with fresh lettuce or whipped cream.

Sea Foam Salad

Ingredients:

2 pkgs of lime Jell-O®

2 cups of boiling water

4 tbsp grated onion

4 tbsp grated carrots

1 cup of whipping cream

1 cup of cottage cheese

1/2 celery, diced

1 cup of salad dressing

Instructions:

Mix Jell-O® and boiling water completely and cool. Add the vegetables, cottage cheese, and salad

dressing. Whip the cream or use Cool Whip®. Put into a mould.

Let the salad set until firm in the fridge.

This makes a very large salad, so more that one mould may have to be used.

Velvet Seafood Salad

Ingredients:

20 oz loaf sandwich bread

butter

plastic bag

4 chopped hard-boiled eggs

1 bunch of chopped green onions

2 cups of mayonnaise (not Miracle Whip®)

1 cup of diced celery

1 can of crabmeat and 2 cans of shrimp

Instructions:

Take the crusts off the loaf of bread. Butter both sides and cut into cubes. Put in a plastic bag with the eggs and onions. Toss and refrigerate overnight.

Next day add: mayonnaise; celery; crab and shrimp meat. Chill for two or three hours, then serve.

Perfection Salad

2 tbsp gelatine

1/2 cup of cold water

1/2 cup of mild vinegar

2 tbsp lemon juice

2 cups boiling water

1 tsp salt

1/2 cup of sugar

2 cups of celery

1 cup of finely shredded cabbage

2 pimentos, minced

Add vinegar, lemon juice, boiling water, salt, and sugar to soaked gelatine. Strain, chill, and add remaining ingredients. When the mixture begins to set, put into the mould. When set cut into pieces.

Makes 12 servings.

** Any mixture of vegetables will do.

Fruit Salad

Ingredients:

Salad:

6 oranges

6 bananas

2 apples

1 can pineapple, chunks

Dressing:

1/2 cup of sugar

1/2 cup of hot water

3 eggs yolks (beaten)

1-2 lemons

whipped cream

Instructions:

For salad:

Prepare the fruit by cutting up and taking the core out of the apples. Serve with dressing.

For dressing:

Boil the sugar and water in a double boiler and pour over egg yolks. Cook until slightly thick. Cool, then add the lemon juice. Thin the mixture with whipped cream.

Chinese Broccoli Salad

Ingredients:

Salad:

2 bunches of fresh broccoli

10 cups of water

2 tbsp oil

1 tbsp salt

Sauce:

2 tbsp light soy sauce

2 tbsp white vinegar

2 tbsp sesame oil

1/4 tsp salt

1 tbsp sugar

Instructions:

Cut the broccoli's flowerets into bite-sized pieces. Peel tough skin from stem and quarter lengthwise. Slant wise cut into 1/4 two-inch pieces. Boil water, oil and salt. Add broccoli and boil quickly for one minute. Drain and rinse in cold water and take a cup towel to dry. Prepare sauce and pour over the broccoli in a dish. Toss to coat the flowerets.

Lettuce Rolls

Ingredients:

softened cream cheese with chopped nuts

pimentos

large leaves of Iceberg lettuce

salt to taste

Instructions:

Spread the lettuce with cream cheese mixture. Salt to taste. Put a strip of pimento across leaf until at the beginning of fold. Roll lettuce at core of leaf. Place rolls in refrigerator for 1-1/2 to 2 hours. Cut across rolls in inch sections.

These go well with a cold salad plate.

OLD FASHIONED DESSERTS FROM
1887

Tory Pudding and Liberal Sauce

Ingredients:

1 cup white flour

1/2 cup white sugar

2 tsp baking powder

1/2 cup raisins

1/2 cup of milk

Instructions:

Sift the flour, sugar, and baking powder and mix them well with the raisins and the milk. Put into a greased baking dish. For the sauce mix 1 cup of brown sugar, 2 cups of boiling water, and 1 tbsp of butter. Put the sauce over the first mixture and bake 30-40 minutes in a 350°F oven.

Blueberry Cottage Pudding

Ingredients:

1 cup of flour

1/2 cup of sugar

2-3 tsp baking powder

pinch of salt

1 cup of blueberries

1 egg

1/4 cup of shortening

1/2 tsp vanilla

1/2 cup of milk

Instructions:

Mix like a cake. Sprinkle a small amount of flour on the berries and add last. Bake at 350°F. For half an hour. Serve plain or with Sweet Brown Sauce.

Sweet Brown Sauce

Ingredients:

2 tbsp butter

1/4 tsp salt

1 cup of boiling water

2 tbsp flour

1/3 cup of brown sugar

1/4 tsp vanilla

Instructions:

Melt the butter and add the flour until it is smooth. Add sugar and stir continually. Remove from heat and put water in. Put on the stove again and bring to the boiling point. At this point add vanilla. Serve hot.

Spiced Peach Squares

Ingredients:

1 cup of sugar

1/3 cup of butter

2 eggs

1-1/2 cups of sifted cake flour

1 tsp baking powder

1/2 tsp salt

1/3 cup of milk

1 tsp of vanilla

1/4 tsp almond extract

sliced peaches

1/2 tsp cinnamon

Instructions:

Cream sugar and butter together. Next add eggs and mix well. Add milk alternating with flour that has been sifted with baking powder and salt. Mix again. Add vanilla and almond extracts. In a 9-inch pan alternate layers between well drained peaches and batter. On the top, dot with butter and put 1/3 cup of sugar and 1/2 tsp of cinnamon. Bake for 40 minutes in a 375°F oven. When done cut in squares and put whipped cream on them.

Coconut Pumpkin Pie

Ingredients:

1 unbaked 9" pie shell

2 eggs

2/3 cup brown sugar

1/2 cup flaked coconut

1/2 tsp salt

1/8 tsp of mace or nutmeg

3/4 tsp cinnamon

1/2 tsp ginger

1 tsp grated lemon or orange rind

1 tsp vanilla

1-1/2 cups of pumpkin

1-1/4 cup of hot milk

2 tbsp butter

Instructions:

Fit pastry into a 9-inch pie plate. Sprinkle with a tsp of flour. Chill.

Preheat oven to 425°F. Beat eggs slightly and combine with the next 8 ingredients. Blend in the pumpkin. Take hot milk and butter and mix into pumpkin mixture. Pour the pie into the pastry and bake in a hot oven for 15 minutes.

After that cook at 350°F for around 35 minutes. Take a silver knife and insert it into the pie to see if it is done. If the knife comes out clean, then it is cooked enough. After the pie has cooled or is slightly warm, serve with whipped cream.

Blueberry Pudding

Ingredients:

1 cup of milk

1/2 tsp soda

1 cup of molasses

2 cups of blueberries

flour to make a rather thick batter

Instructions:

Dissolve soda in the milk; add molasses, blueberries, and flour enough to make a batter. Put these ingredients in a coffee can or clean metal can with tin foil over the top. Secure the tin foil with a string. Put in a large pot with enough water so it won't run dry.

Take the cover and put it on the pot. Steam for 2 hours.

After-Thought Pudding

Ingredients:

2 cups of apple sauce

2 egg yolks

butter for dish

whites of eggs

1/2 cup of white sugar

Instructions:

Take the apple sauce and egg yolks and mix together. Put it in a buttered dish and bake for 10-15 minutes. Beat the egg whites stiff and add the sugar. Spread the meringue on top and put in the oven at 350°F to bake golden brown.

Bird's Nest Pudding

Ingredients:

6 peeled and cored apples

sugar

2 cups of milk

2 tbsp flour

3 eggs

Instructions:

Put some sugar in the holes of the apples (enough to fill the holes), after putting the fruit in an oven-proof dish. Make a batter with the milk, flour, and eggs. Pour this onto the apples and bake until they are soft.

Raspberry Charlotte

Ingredients:

dry bread crumbs

butter

ripe raspberries

sugar

Butter an oven proof dish and cover the bottom with bread crumbs. Next put a layer of raspberries and sprinkle with some sugar. Make alternating layers of bread crumbs and raspberries, using half the quantity of crumbs as raspberries.

Dot the top with butter and bake with a Pyrex® plate over the mixture for half an hour in a 350°F oven. Take the plate off and bake until golden brown. Whipped cream can be served with this pudding.

Raspberry Custard Pudding

Ingredients

2 cups of milk, boiling

2 tbsp cornstarch

small amount of cold milk

2 eggs, beaten

1/2 cup of sugar

raspberry jam

Instructions:

Put the cornstarch which has been moistened with a little bit of cold milk into the boiling milk. Add 2 eggs and the sugar. Put 1 cup of raspberry jam in the bottom of the dish and pour the custard over it.

Eat warm, but not hot. Cream and sugar can be added.

Miss Polly Dana's Pudding

Ingredients:

1/4 lbs of rice

4 cups of milk

1 stick of cinnamon

1/4 lbs of butter

sugar to taste

1/2 nutmeg, grated

little bit of water

small amount of Rose water

5 beaten eggs

Instructions:

Cook the rice in the boiling milk and cinnamon. When it thick, pour it into a pan and stir in the butter and sugar to taste. Grate in nutmeg and add Rose water. Mix together well and add eggs. Butter an oven proof dish and pour the pudding into it. Bake until golden brown. Puff paste may be put on the

top.

Oxford Pudding

Ingredients:

4 large, tart apples

water

1 tbsp melted butter

1/2 cup of sugar

1/2 cup of fine bread crumbs

4 egg yolks

2 eggs beaten

Instructions:

Peel and core the apples and boil in so little water, that when it is done, no water remains. Mash and add butter, sugar, bread crumbs, the yolks of 4 eggs and the whites of 2 eggs beaten light. Put into a baking dish and cover with the whites of 2 eggs and 1 cup of sugar. Bake until golden brown in a moderate oven (350°F).

MORE DESSERTS

Rich Honey Gingerbread

Ingredients:

1-1/2 cups of sifted flour

1/4 cup of sugar

2 tsp baking powder

1/4 tsp baking soda

1/2 tsp salt

1/2 tsp ginger

1/2 tsp cinnamon

1/2 tsp cloves

1 egg, well beaten

1/2 cup of honey

1/2 cup of milk or water

4 tbsp melted shortening

Instructions:

Sift dry ingredients together 3 times. Mix egg, honey, milk and shortening. Combine liquid and dry ingredients and beat well. Pour into greased pan and bake at 350°F for 30-35 minutes. Makes a 9" x 12" cake.

* Substitute cooking oil for shortening if health is a concern.

Orange Marmalade Gingerbread

Ingredients:

1-3/4 cup sifted cake flour

3/4 tsp baking powder

1/2 tsp baking soda

1 tsp cinnamon

1 tsp ginger

1/2 tsp salt

3 tbsp shortening (or cooking oil)

1 egg well beaten

1/2 cup of molasses

1 cup of orange marmalade

4 tbsp boiling water

Instructions:

Sift flour, baking powder, soda, cinnamon, ginger, and salt together. Cream shortening. Add egg and mix well. Add molasses and marmalade and beat well. Add sifted dry ingredients and hot water alternately in small amounts, beating after each addition. Pour into greased pan and bake at 350°F for 25-30 minutes. Makes an 8" x 8" cake.

Sweet Potato Cake

Instructions:

1-1/2 cups of sifted flour

2 tsp of baking powder

1/2 cup of shortening

2 eggs, well beaten

2 cups of hot, mashed sweet potatoes

3/4 cup of sugar

1/4 tsp salt

1 tsp cinnamon or nutmeg

1/2 cup of milk

juice of 1/2 lemon

Instructions:

Sift flour and baking powder together. Add shortening and beaten eggs to potatoes while still hot. Add sugar, salt, and nutmeg and beat well. Add flour and milk alternately in small amounts, mixing well after each addition. Add lemon juice. Pour into greased loaf pan and bake at 325°F for one hour. Makes an 8" x 4" cake.

* If you feel that shortening isn't healthy you can use cooking oil, which will give the cake a denser texture. Don't use olive oil   because it would make the cake heavy.

Apple Snow

Ingredients:

5 large, tart apples cored and quartered

juice and zest of one lemon

1/2 cup of sugar

3 eggs separated

2 cups of milk

Instructions:

Peel the apples and steam them until they are soft. Rub them through a sieve. When cool, add the lemon juice and zest, sugar, and the whites of the eggs. Beat to a froth and pile in a glass dish. Boil 2 cups of milk and stir into it the yolks of three eggs beaten with 3 tbsps of sugar. Serve the custard with the snow.

Coconut pudding

Ingredients:

2 cups of milk

1 tsp butter

very small grated coconut

3 eggs, beaten

1/2 cup of sugar

pinch of salt

pastry

Instructions:

Boil one pint of milk with 1 tsp of butter in it. Pour it over the coconut. When cooled, add the eggs; sugar; and salt.

Have a deep pie plate lined with pastry and pour the mixture into it. Bake until the pudding is set.

Cherry Cake

Ingredients:

1/2 lbs of flour

5 oz of sugar

6 oz of fat (shortening, margarine, butter)

small 1/2 Tsp of baking powder

3 eggs

6 oz pitted cherries

Instructions:

Cream the fat and sugar together. Sift the flour and add the eggs. Add baking powder with the last of the flour. Cut cherries in half and mix well with flour. Have the mixture fairly stiff to hold the cherries in. Turn into a greased pan and bake at 350°F for 1-1/2 to 2 hours.

Christmas Pudding

Ingredients:

1 lbs of bread crumbs

1 lbs of seedless raisins

1 lbs of currents

1/2 lbs of citron, cut in small pieces

1/2 lbs of suet, butter, or margarine

1/4 lbs of sugar

1 tsp salt

1 tsp clove

2 tsp of cinnamon

1/2 tsp of mace or nutmeg

juice and zest of one lemon

6 yolks of eggs, beaten

large cup of milk

Instructions:

Mix all ingredients together and add the egg yolks and milk. Next add the beaten egg whites. Boil in a buttered mold for six hours. Serve with Foaming Sauce.

* A coffee can or two can be used as a pan. Make sure that you use a large pot and that there is enough water in it, so it won't boil dry. Put tin foil over the can and tie it with string. Lastly, put a lid on the pot and boil. Keep and eye on it so that it won't boil dry.

Almond Rice

Ingredients:

2 tbsp rice

boiling water

pinch of salt

1/2 pint of cream

3 tbsp sugar

vanilla extract

blanched and browned almonds

Instructions:

Wash the rice and cook for 20 minutes with a pinch of salt. Strain and make sure the rice grains separate. Beat 1/2 pint of cream stiffly. Add sugar, rice, and vanilla extract. After the almonds are roasted in the oven, chop them, and mix them with the rice and cream.

Lemon Delight

Ingredients:

2 oz of margarine

1 teacup castor sugar

2 tbsp Self rising flour

pinch of salt

rind and juice of 2 lemons

2 eggs

Instructions:

Beat margarine and sugar. Add lemon zest and juice. Next add egg yolks, flour, and milk. Beat well.

Fold in whipped egg whites and put in a pie plate or casserole dish. Place in a metal pan with cold water coming half-way up the casserole dish. Bake at 350°F for 45 minutes to an hour.

www.ingramcontent.com/pod-product-compliance
Lightning Source LLC
Chambersburg PA
CBHW051044030426
42339CB00006B/184